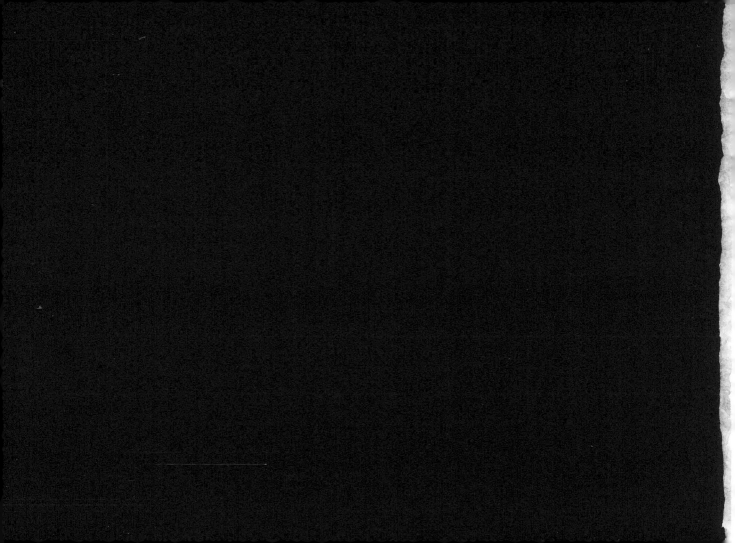

Cattitudes

VICTORIA ROBERTS

imagine! Publishing

AN IMAGINE BOOK

Published by Charlesbridge

85 Main Street, Watertown, MA 02472

(617) 926-0329

www.charlesbridge.com

Printed in China, September 2013.

Library of Congress Cataloging-in-Publication Data is available on request

ISBN 978-1-62354-023-4

2 4 6 8 10 9 7 5 3 1

For information about custom editions, special sales, premium and corporate purchases,
please contact Charlesbridge Publishing at specialsales@charlesbridge.com

For Shirley A. Wright

Cats of Singular Talent

HENRY & ANAÏS

FRIDA KAHLO

MERCE

EMILY DICKINSON &
ELIZABETH BISHOP

MARIANNE MOORE

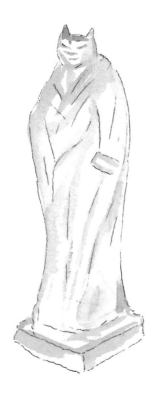

RODIN

14

MATISSE

15

AGED 5   AGED 25

ANDY

Cats of the Cloth

RASTA

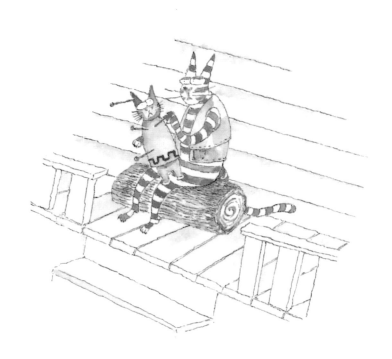

WHIRLING
DERVISHES

25

MONKS

NOVICES

FOUR CARDINALS

1/2 DOZEN NUNS,
BAREFOOT

Self-Portraits

SELF-PORTRAIT
NO. 57, ORIGAMI

32

SELF-PORTRAIT
NO. 72, TOPIARY

33

SELF-PORTRAIT
NO. 33, CATWARE

SELF-PORTRAIT
NO. 14, IN A BOWL
OF CREAM

35

SELF-PORTRAIT
NO. 54, T-SHIRT

SELF-PORTRAIT
NOS. 74 THROUGH
642, BOOTH

37

Mad Cats

JANUARY

FEBRUARY

MARCH

APRIL

MAY

JUNE

JULY

AUGUST

ANALYSIS

SEPTEMBER

OCTOBER

NOVEMBER

DECEMBER

ART THERAPY

PROZAC

GROUP

47

Small Pleasures

SMALL PLEASURE
NO. 18, FALCONRY

SMALL PLEASURE
NO. 1, LOX

SMALL PLEASURE
NO. 37, SIAMESE
SEWING CIRCLE

SMALL PLEASURE
NO. 2, WOOL

58

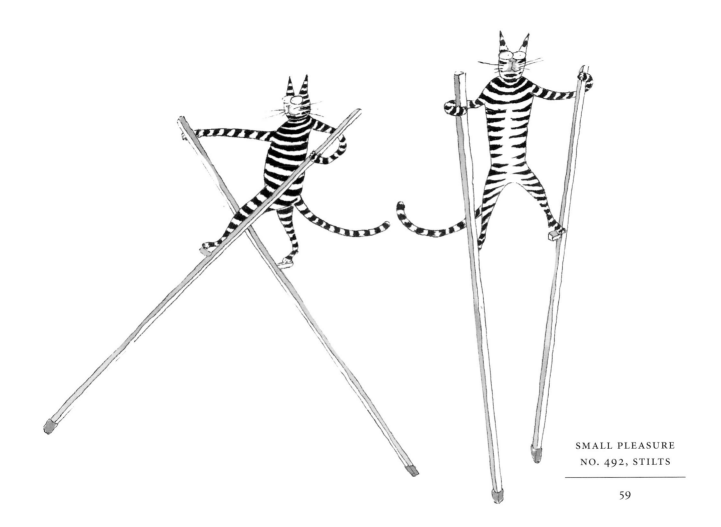

SMALL PLEASURE
NO. 492, STILTS

SMALL PLEASURE
NO. 35, BEEKEEPING

SMALL PLEASURE
NO. 49,
BOOK-OF-THE-
MONTH CLUB

63

SMALL PLEASURE
NO. 119, BAGPIPES

SMALL PLEASURE
NO. 29,
VENTRILOQUISM

Cats in Costume

CHILE, ARGENTINA,
URUGUAY

74

SPAIN

76

Beauty Cats

BEAUTY PARLOR

CAT HOSE

CAT WAX

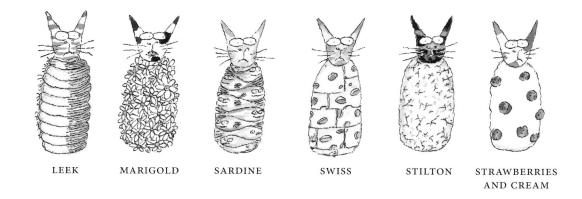

LEEK   MARIGOLD   SARDINE   SWISS   STILTON   STRAWBERRIES
AND CREAM

CAT WRAPS

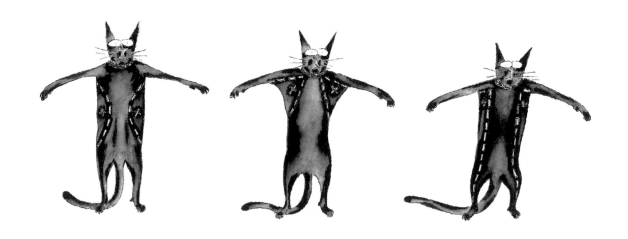

CAT TUCKS I & II

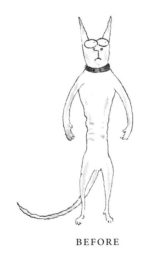

BEFORE   AFTER